Jake Drake

KNOW-IT-ALL

Andrew Clements

Jake Drake
KNOW-IT-ALL

Cover illustration by Marla Frazee

Interior illustrations by Janet Pedersen

Houghton Mifflin Edition

Printed in the United States of America

ISBN-13: 978-0-547-07367-5
ISBN-10: 0-547-07367-4

14   1083 15 14 13
4500402030

Contents

CHAPTER ONE

The Catch

I'm Jake, Jake Drake. I'm in fourth grade, and I'm ten years old. And I have to tell the truth about something: I've been crazy about computers all my life.

My first computer was an old Mac Classic with a black-and-white screen. I got to play Reader Rabbit and Magic Math. I got to draw pictures on the screen, and I played Battle Tanks. And that was before I could even read.

Then our family got a Mac with a big color monitor. And I got to play Tetris and Shanghai and Solitaire and Spectre. Then I got a joystick for Christmas when I was four, and so did my best friend, Willie. Whenever Willie came to my house we played computer games together. It's not like we played computers all the time, because my mom made a one-hour-a-day rule at my house. But Willie and I filled up that hour almost every day.

Then the computers started getting super-fast, and I started messing around with Virtual Drummer, and then SimCity, and SimAnt, and PGA Golf, and about ten other games. And then the Internet arrived at my house, and all of a sudden I could make my computer do some pretty amazing stuff. It was like a magic window.

I'm telling all of this because if I don't, then the rest of this story makes me look like a real jerk. And I'm not a jerk, not most of the time. I just really like computers.

When I started kindergarten, there was a computer in our room. When the teacher saw I was good on it, I got to use it. I even got to teach other kids how to use it. Except for Kevin and

Marsha. They didn't want me to tell them about computers or anything else.

Like I said before, I'm ten now, so I've had some time to figure out some stuff. And one thing I know for sure is this: There's nothing worse than a know-it-all.

Don't get me wrong. I'm pretty smart, and I like being smart. And almost all the kids I know, they're pretty smart, too.

But some kids, they have to prove they're smart. Like, all the time. And not just smart. They have to be the smartest. And that's what Marsha and Kevin are like.

Marsha McCall and Kevin Young were nice enough kids back in kindergarten—as long as I didn't try to tell them anything about the computer. Because when I tried to show Kevin how to make shapes with the drawing program, he said, "I know that." But I don't think he really did. And when I tried to show Marsha how to print out a picture of a kitten, she said, "I can do that myself."

But a lot of the time Kevin and Marsha were pretty nice because kindergarten was mostly playtime.

But when we got to first grade, school changed. All of a sudden there were right answers and wrong answers. And Kevin and Marsha, they went nuts about getting the right answers.

But it was worse than that. They both wanted to get the right answer *first*. It was like they thought school was a TV game show. If you get the right answer first, you win the big prize. Anyway, they both turned into know-it-alls.

Our first-grade teacher was Miss Grimes. Every time she asked a question, Marsha would start shaking all over and waving her hand around and whispering really loud, like this: "Ooh, ooh! I know! I know! I know!"

And while Marsha was going, "Ooh, ooh," Kevin looked like his arm was going to pull his whole body right out of his chair and drag it up to the ceiling, like his arm had its own brain or something.

It was pretty awful. But Miss Grimes, she liked it when Kevin and Marsha tried to be the best at everything. She liked seeing who could get done first with a math problem. She liked

letting everyone with a hundred on a spelling quiz line up first for lunch or recess. First grade felt like a big contest, and Miss Grimes smiled at the winners and frowned at the losers.

When she asked the class a question, most of the time Miss Grimes called on Marsha first. If Marsha was slow or didn't know something, then Kevin got a turn. If Kevin messed up, then she would call on someone else.

And I think I know why Miss Grimes always called on Marsha and Kevin. I think it's because she's kind of a know-it-all herself. I bet she was just like Marsha back when she was in first grade.

Second grade wasn't much better. The only good thing was that my second-grade teacher wasn't like Miss Grimes. Mrs. Brattle didn't want school to be a big contest. So she hardly ever called on the know-it-alls.

All year long, Mrs. Brattle kept saying stuff like, "Kevin and Marsha, please look around at all the other students in this class. They have good ideas, too. Just put your hands down for now."

That didn't stop Kevin and Marsha. The "ooh-oohing" and the arm waving never let up.

But last year, when I was in third grade, that's when things got out of control. And I guess it was partly my fault.

And Mrs. Snavin, my third-grade teacher? She had something to do with it. And so did the principal, Mrs. Karp.

And so did this guy named Mr. Lenny Cordo over at Wonky's Super Computer Store. He had *a lot* to do with it.

Because Mr. Lenny Cordo came to my school one day back when I was in third grade. And Mr. Lenny Cordo told me that he had a present for me. Something really wonderful. Something I had been wishing for.

But there was one small catch. Because there's always at least one small catch.

And this was the catch: Before Mr. Lenny Cordo could give me this wonderful thing that I wanted so much, I would have to do something.

I would have to turn myself into Jake Drake, Know-It-All.

CHAPTER TWO

Big News

When something big is going to happen at school, the kids are always the last to know. First the principal and the teachers and the other grown-ups get everything figured out. Then they tell me and my friends about it. Which doesn't seem very fair, but that's how it happens.

So one Tuesday morning before Christmas vacation, there was an assembly for the kids in third grade, fourth grade, and fifth grade. I sat up front with all the other third graders.

The principal looked huge. Mrs. Karp is

always tall. But standing up on the stage that morning in a green dress, she looked like a giant piece of celery.

There was someone else on the stage. It was this man I had never seen before. He was wearing a yellow sport coat and a purple tie with green polka dots. It was the first time I had ever seen a yellow sport coat. Or a purple tie with green polka dots. I thought maybe he worked for a circus.

He sat on a folding chair, and he had a wide roll of paper lying across his lap. It was noisy in the auditorium. Then Mrs. Karp held up two fingers and leaned toward the microphone.

Mrs. Karp should not be allowed to have a microphone. She doesn't need one. Every kid in the school knows how loud she can yell. When Mrs. Karp yells, it feels like the tiles are going to peel up off the floor and start flying around.

No one wanted to hear Mrs. Karp yell, and especially not into a microphone. So it got quiet in about one second.

Mrs. Karp said, "Good morning, students."

And then she paused.

So all of us said, "Good morning, Mrs. Karp."

Then Mrs. Karp said, "I have some good news this morning. The people at Wonky's Super Computer Store have been talking to our Board of Education. And in just one month, our school is going to have twenty brand-new computers for our media center. *Twenty* new computers—isn't that wonderful?"

Mrs. Karp paused, so all the kids and the teachers in the audience clapped. Some of the fifth graders started cheering and shouting stuff like, "Yaaay!" and, "All riiight!" and, "*Awe*some!"

So Mrs. Karp had to hold up two fingers again. It got quiet right away.

Then she said, "But there's a reason that I've asked just the third-, fourth-, and fifth-grade classes to come here this morning. And that's because during the next-to-last week of January our school is going to have a science fair!"

Mrs. Karp paused again.

But no one clapped this time.

Then she said, "This is the first time we've had a science fair at Despres Elementary School, so this is something brand-new for all of us. And to tell you more about our very first science fair ever, I'd like to introduce Mr. Lenny Cordo. He's the manager of Wonky's Super Computer Store. Mr. Cordo."

The man in the yellow sport coat and the purple tie with green polka dots stood up. He forgot he had that roll of paper on his lap. It dropped onto the floor and rolled off the front of the stage. A lot of kids started laughing. Then Mrs. Karp moved back toward the microphone, and the laughing stopped.

Mrs. Snavin got up from her chair in the front row. She picked up the wide roll of paper and handed it back to the man.

Mr. Lenny Cordo was a lot shorter than Mrs. Karp, so he had to pull the microphone down. Then he said, "Thank you, Mrs. Karp. I am so glad to be here."

That's what Mr. Cordo said, but he didn't look that way. There was sweat all over his forehead, and the roll of paper in his hands was shaking. I guess we looked scary. So he talked fast to get it over with.

"At Wonky's Super Computer Store, we love kids. At Wonky's Super Computer Store, we think it's never too early to get kids excited about science and computers and the future. And that's why Wonky's Super Computer Store is proud to sponsor the First Annual Despres Elementary School Science Fair."

And that's when Mr. Cordo held up the wide piece of paper and let it unroll. It was a banner. It said WONKY'S FIRST ANNUAL ELEMENTARY SCHOOL SCIENCE FAIR.

The biggest word on the banner was "WONKY'S." And the whole banner was upside down.

There was a little laughing, but it stopped because Mr. Cordo kept talking. He wasn't scared anymore. Now he sounded like a guy selling cars on TV.

"In the real world, the world where all of you will live and learn and work in the future, people get rewards for doing good work. And that is why Wonky's Super Computer Store is offering a GRAND PRIZE for the best science fair project in grade three, grade four, and grade five!"

When you say those two words, "GRAND PRIZE," kids pay attention. It got so quiet, I

could almost hear the sweat sliding down Mr. Cordo's forehead. He saw we were listening now, so he took his time.

"That's right. There will be *three* grand prizes for the First Annual Wonky's Science Fair. And do you want to know what each grand prize will be?"

With one giant voice, every kid in the auditorium shouted, "YES!"

So Mr. Cordo leaned closer to the microphone and shouted back. "Then I'm going to tell you! The grand prize for the best science fair project in grade three, grade four, and grade five will be . . . a brand-new Hyper-Cross-Functional Bluntium Twelve computer system!"

I couldn't believe it! For the past three months, the Bluntium Twelve computer had been advertised on every TV channel. And in every magazine and newspaper. I had seen it on billboards and even on the side of a bus.

The Bluntium Twelve was the computer I had been begging my mom and dad to get. It was the fastest computer with the coolest games and the best connections.

It was the computer of my dreams.

All around me kids were clapping and saying stuff like, "Great!" and, "Cool!" and, "Yeah!"

And then I noticed Kevin, and then Marsha. They were sitting in my row of seats.

Kevin and Marsha were not clapping. They were not talking.

Kevin and Marsha were sitting very still. They were thinking.

They were already planning how to win that Bluntium Twelve computer—*my* computer!

And when Mrs. Karp quieted everyone down, I kept looking around, and I could see that other kids were doing the same thing. Kids were starting to think and plan.

Mrs. Karp said some other stuff, but I didn't listen. I was thinking, too.

Because I saw that the only thing standing between me and my very own, superfast, supercool computer was about a hundred other third-grade brains.

But I had a feeling that the only other brains I really had to worry about belonged to those two know-it-alls—Kevin Young and Marsha McCall.

CHAPTER THREE

The Rules

After the assembly about the science fair, our classroom was noisy.

Mrs. Snavin came in and said, "Everyone please sit in your chairs. I have something to give you."

Eric Kenner said, "Is it a computer?"

Everybody laughed, even Mrs. Snavin.

She said, "No, it's not a computer, Eric. But it *is* some news about the science fair."

That got things quiet fast.

"Now," said Mrs. Snavin, "the first thing you all need to know is that no one has to be part of the science fair. This is something you can choose to do, or choose not to do. It will be good experience, but it will not make any difference in your grades either way."

While she was talking, Mrs. Snavin took a pile of papers from her desk and started passing them out.

She said, "This is about the science fair. You should take this booklet home and read it with your mom or dad. There is a form that you and a parent will have to sign. Bring it back to me before Christmas vacation if you are going to enter the science fair. You should pay special attention to page three. That's the page that tells the kinds of projects that are allowed, and the kinds of projects you should not make."

It was dead quiet in the room except for the rustling of paper.

I got my booklet and started to flip through it. It had ten pages, and it all looked pretty boring. I started to fold it up so I could put it in my back-pack to take home.

But then I looked at Kevin. He was hunched over his desk, reading fast. He had a pencil and

he was making little check marks and notes on the pages.

Then I turned my head toward the other side of the room and looked at Marsha. Same thing, except she was using a pink Hi-Liter.

Usually, I would have looked at Marsha and Kevin and said to myself, *know-it-alls*.

But not that day. I grabbed my red pen, I unfolded my science fair papers, and I started reading. No way was I going to let either of those kids get my Bluntium Twelve computer.

Then Mrs. Snavin said, "Are there any questions about the science fair?"

Right away Kevin's hand went up.

Mrs. Snavin said, "Yes, Kevin?"

"Can kids work together on the science fair?"

Mrs. Snavin started flipping pages in the information packet. She said, "On page nine it says, 'Students may work on a science fair project alone or with one partner.'"

Then I put my hand up. Mrs. Snavin nodded at me, so I said, "But what if two kids make a project, and it wins first place. Would both kids get a prize?"

Mrs. Snavin flipped some more pages. Then she said, "On page six it says, 'Only one grand prize will be awarded for the winning project in grade three, grade four, and grade five.' So the answer is no, Jake. If a team won first place, I guess they would have to figure out how to share the prize or split it up someway."

So that was that. I had to work by myself. No way was I going to split my new computer with anybody else.

Mrs. Snavin said, "Any other questions?"

Two more kids put up their hands—Pete Morris and Marsha. Marsha got called on first.

Whenever Marsha talked, everything sounded like a question.

She said, "On page seven? Well, it says I have to get my project idea approved? Before I start working on it? Well, what if I want to start working on it today? Like, after school today? And tonight?" Mrs. Snavin smiled. "I think you'd better wait until you talk with your mom or dad before you begin, Marsha. And don't worry. There will be plenty of time."

You see that? How Mrs. Snavin said "there will

be plenty of time"? And how she said "don't worry"? That's because Mrs. Snavin didn't get it. She didn't understand how know-it-alls have to get the right answer. Or about how they always have to be first. Or how they always worry.

Pete Morris still had his hand up. So Mrs. Snavin called on him.

Pete's a science kid. He knows every kind of bug there is. Even their fancy names, and which bug is related to which other bug, and what they eat and how long they live. Pete's really smart.

Pete said, "I think insects would be a good science fair topic. Because I have a lot of different bugs. Bugs are my hobby. And rocks, too. And also worms and plants. And sometimes different kinds of monkeys. So, is it okay to have your science fair project and your hobby be the same thing?"

Mrs. Snavin said, "That's a good question, Pete, and the answer is yes. But I still think you all need to talk to your moms or dads, and they can help you decide what's best for you to do. Now, that's all the time we have for this today."

Then it was quiet reading time, so we all put

the science fair stuff away and got out our library books.

Except I didn't. And neither did Marsha. She put the science fair papers down in her lap where she could keep reading them.

And I didn't even bother to look over at Kevin. I knew he was still thinking about the science fair, too.

And me? I kept the papers out on my desk. That way I could look down at them under my library book. I needed to get to work. Maybe I could go to the library after lunch. Then I could get a head start.

Because I wanted to be the first. And the best. I wanted to win.

And I didn't just want to win. I *had* to win.

I had to be know-it-all number one.

CHAPTER FOUR

Hunters

By lunchtime, I had read everything about the science fair. Twice. I was ready to work.

So I waited until just before lunch. I waited until Mrs. Snavin was alone at her desk. Then I went up and asked for a library pass for after lunch. And I kind of whispered. And when she gave me the pass, I hid it in my hand.

But Marsha saw it anyway. Because Marsha was watching me like a cat watches a hamster. And right away, she jumped up and rushed over to the teacher's desk. She said, "Mrs. Snavin?

A library pass? Could I have one, too?"

Except Marsha didn't whisper. So three seconds later, Kevin also had a library pass.

Because that's the way it is, and you have to get used to it. Know-it-alls are usually copycats, too.

After lunch, the library was like a know-it-all convention. All the smart kids were there. Plus all the kids who thought they were smart. Plus all the kids who wanted everyone else to think they were smart. Plus me.

We were all there. Everyone wanted a head start. Everyone wanted to win.

The only good thing was that not all the kids there were in third grade. Besides me and Marsha and Kevin, there were only three other third graders.

And Pete Morris wasn't one of them. I looked out the window and I saw Pete. He was out by the bushes near the fence. He was bending over. He was looking at one of the branches.

But my best friend, Willie, was in the library. His real name is Phil, but his last name is Willis, so everyone calls him Willie, even his teachers. Willie's third-grade teacher was Mrs. Frule.

When Willie saw me, he smiled and came over to my table. "Hey," he said, "isn't it great? I mean about the computer? I would love to have that thing in my room. Got any good ideas yet? I think I might try to build a bridge or something like that, you know? Something big. How about you? What do you want to do?"

But all I said was, "Listen, Willie, I've got to get to work now, okay?"

"Sure," said Willie, "but I thought maybe we could be partners. We could make something totally . . . you know, like, totally . . . total."

Willie was great at starting sentences. Finishing them was the hard part.

I shook my head. "Won't work, Willie. What if what we make wins first prize? Then what?"

Willie looked at me like I was nuts. "Then we'll have this cool computer, that's what. We can keep it at your house some of the time, and at my house some of the time. It'll be great!"

I shook my head again. "I don't think so, Willie. I think we better just do our own stuff."

Willie shrugged. "Okay. But if I win, I'll still let you use my computer sometimes, okay?"

I smiled and said, "Sure. That'll be great."

But inside, to myself, I said, *You? Win the science fair? Forget about it, Willie. That grand prize is* mine.

Which was not very nice. But when you have to get the right answer, and you have to get it first, and you have to win, then you don't have as much time to be nice anymore.

When Willie walked away, I looked at the papers about the science fair again. There was a part that said you couldn't make a project that used fire or acid. For electricity, you could only use batteries. And you couldn't use chemicals that might explode or make smoke.

Those rules knocked a lot of fun stuff off the list.

In the booklet it said there would be five judges. So I tried to think like a science fair judge. But I got tired of that. It was hard enough to think like a third grader.

I grabbed my papers and went over to a computer that was hooked up to the Internet. I sat down, clicked on "search," and then typed in "science fair projects."

In two seconds, I got a message. It said 206,996 Web pages matched with my search! And the first ten links were on the screen.

So I clicked on a link that said "Science Fair Helper." Sounded like the right stuff. And it was. It had some good things, so I clicked on a second link. And that second link had some good ideas, too. And so did the third link, and the fourth, and the fifth.

Then it hit me—there was probably a good idea on every page, all 206,996 of them! But I didn't need 200,000 ideas. I just needed one. I needed *my* idea.

I felt something. Behind me. I turned around real quick, and guess what? It was Kevin Young. He had come up right behind me and he was staring at the screen. My screen.

"Hey!" I said. "What are you doing, Kevin?"

Kevin shrugged. "Nothing."

I said, "Then go do nothing somewhere else."

Kevin had red hair, and his face was freckled, and his eyes were this real pale blue. And he didn't blink much.

Kevin stuck out his chin and said, "I can be anywhere I want to in the library. And you know, it's against the rules to copy a project from the Internet."

And from around the end of some shelves, suddenly Marsha was standing there next to Kevin. She nodded her head so her ponytail bobbed up and down. "That's right, what Kevin said? About copying? How it's, like, cheating?"

It was hard not to get mad. Real mad.

But all I said was, "What? Do you think I'm stupid? I know not to cheat. Just mind your own business, both of you. You know what things look like right now? It looks like you two are copying ideas from *me*, that's what it looks like."

They left, and I was still pretty mad.

But when I thought about it later, I felt better . . . about Kevin and Marsha watching out for me, I mean. I was something they weren't so sure about. It made me feel good because if they were worried about me, that meant I was worth worrying about.

Jake Drake was something those know-it-alls didn't know about, and they both knew it.

CHAPTER FIVE

K-I-A/D-I-A

That night after dinner I told my mom and dad about the science fair. We were having ice cream for dessert. Mom and I had chocolate, and Dad and Abby had vanilla and strawberry. Abby's my little sister. She's two years younger than I am. So back then, when I was in third grade, Abby was a first grader.

I handed the science fair booklet to my dad. Right away he flipped through it. He looked at each page for about two seconds.

He said, "Okay . . . yeah . . . that makes

sense . . . this is good . . . fine. Great, Jake. This'll be a lot of fun."

Then he ripped the permission slip off the back page. He signed his name and handed his pen to me. "Just sign on the line, Jake . . . there you go. Now we're all set. So what do you think? You want to make a rocket? Or maybe a volcano? Those are a lot of fun. Or maybe a model of a planet? I always loved making Saturn, you know? The one with all the rings? That's a great project."

Meanwhile, my mom started reading the booklet. Carefully.

Abby wasn't doing anything except stirring her ice cream around and around in her bowl.

Mom said, "My goodness! Jim, did you see that there's a prize for first place?"

"Well, of course . . . well, sure," Dad said. "There's always a prize for first place. When I won my seventh-grade science fair, I got a nice trophy. But I think my sister threw it out when I went to college."

My mom winked at me. Then she said to Dad, "Okay. You know there's a prize. But do you know what the prize is?"

My dad said, "Well . . . no, I mean, not exactly. But I know there's a prize, so we'll try to win it— right, Jakey? Like with a rocket, something really exciting. The judges love exciting projects."

Mom had flipped to another page. She looked sideways at me and said, "Jake, why don't you tell your dad why you will not be making a rocket for the science fair."

I said, "That's because on page three it says I can't make anything that burns, or smokes, or explodes."

Dad said, "Well . . . there *are* other kinds of rockets . . . like the kind that use water power. You know, a water rocket? So, we could still make a rocket."

Mom laughed and said, "That sounds like something a K-I-A/D-I-A might say."

I said, "What's that mean . . . K-I-A/D-I-A?"

Abby looked up from her ice-cream soup. She said, "I know. It means Know-It-All/Do-It-All. Mommy told me."

And I remembered that I had heard Mom say that before.

One time Dad wouldn't read about how to put

a new bicycle together. Mom said he was being a K-I-A/D-I-A.

And when we got a new garage door opener, it broke because Dad hooked the motor on backwards. He didn't read the instructions. When that happened, Mom said, "Dear, sometimes I wish you weren't such a K-I-A/D-I-A."

Or when my dad wouldn't stop and ask for directions when we were lost in the car? I heard Mom say, "Don't be a K-I-A/D-I-A."

Mom handed the booklet back to Dad, and he started reading.

I said, "You know the prize? It's amazing, Dad. If I win first prize, I get a Bluntium Twelve computer! From Wonky's Super Computer Store."

Dad said, "A whole system? A Bluntium Twelve?"

"Yeah," I said, "and a year of free Internet service, too!"

Dad whistled.

And then Abby tried to whistle, too. But instead, some melted ice cream drooled down her chin.

Dad looked at the booklet again. He said,

"Well, I guess we had better get right to work on this, eh, Jake?"

See that? How my dad said "we"? He said, ". . . *We* had better get right to work. . . ."

That "we" got me worried. This was supposed to be *my* science fair. Right in the science fair booklet it said that kids had to do their own work.

And then I thought, *What if Dad thinks he's going to get a new computer when my project wins first prize?*

Kids like Kevin and Marsha? I knew they were going to be a problem. I was ready for that.

But what if your dad is a K-I-A—and a D-I-A, too?

How do you tell your own dad to keep hands off? And that you don't want to share your new computer with anyone—not even him?

On this science fair project, there was only room for one K-I-A.

And that was me.

CHAPTER SIX

What to Do

After dessert, I took the science fair booklet to my room. It had some ideas about choosing what to do.

The rules said I had to use *the scientific method*. Which works like this:

First you look around the world and see something interesting. That's called *observation*.

After you look around, you ask a question about something. That part's called the *question*. Which makes sense.

Then you make a guess about the answer.

When you do a science fair project, your guess is called a *hypothesis*. But it's still a guess.

Then you plan out some trials to test and see if your guess is right or wrong. That part is called the *method*.

Then you do your testing, and you write down what you find out. That's called the *result*.

And then you have to tell if your guess was right or wrong. That's called the *conclusion*.

But I was stuck way back at the beginning. I was having trouble with the question part. So I kept reading and the science fair booklet said:

Try filling in these blanks to make a question you want to explore:

What is the effect of _____ on _____?"

And then it gave two examples:

What is the effect of __dishwasher soap__ on __grass seedlings__?

What is the effect of __total darkness__ on __how much gerbils sleep__?

So I tried filling in some words of my own.

What is the effect of sawdust on the taste of a vanilla milkshake ?

What is the effect of a dead cockroach on Abby's pillow at bedtime ?

What is the effect of a red hot pepper on Willie's peanut butter sandwich ?

I liked my questions.

And after you ask a question, you have to make a guess. So I gave that a try too:

—Sawdust would make a vanilla milkshake taste like . . . plywood?

—A dead cockroach on Abby's pillow at bedtime would . . . cause loud screams and a lot of yelling, and make me be grounded with no TV or computer games for three weeks.

—And a red hot pepper on Willie's peanut butter sandwich would . . . make Willie jump up from his chair, drink six cartons of chocolate milk, and then throw up all over the cafeteria.

Pretty good guesses.

But I had to stop messing around.

So I lay down on my bed and looked at the ceiling. My ceiling has all these swirls and ridges. It's like looking at clouds. Sometimes I can see all kinds of stuff up there. But that night I didn't see anything. Just a big white blank.

Deciding what to do for a science fair is hard. It's hard because what you really have to do is choose what *not* to do.

Because you could do anything. You could do millions of different things.

Except you can only do one thing.

So after you choose all the stuff *not* to do, then you look at what's left over. And that's what you do.

I got up and went over to my dresser and opened the top drawer. It's my junk drawer. That's what my mom calls it because it all looks like junk to her.

And then I got an idea. Maybe I could find an idea by looking at my junk. All of it.

So I grabbed my notebook from my backpack.

I opened it to an empty page. I found a pencil. Then I looked into my junk drawer and I started making a list.

7 paper clips

3 big paper clips

9 old batteries

1 twisty pencil sharpener

1 orange golf ball

1 toenail clippers

2 wooden yo–yos

1 plastic yo–yo with no string

13 rubber bands

4 Hot Wheels

18 baseball cards

6 of Willie's basketball cards

3 pens

29 colored pencils

7 keys that I don't know what they fit

17 crayons

9 marbles

1 plastic magnifying glass

2 mini–superballs

half a pair of dice

1 piece of chain from a broken lamp

1 little lock, no key

1 red magnet shaped like a horseshoe

1 broken glow–in–the–dark watch

1 mini Frisbee

37 pennies

1 empty Altoids tin with 1 Canadian quarter

1 roll of thin wire

1 red stamp pad

1 fingernail file

1 plastic ruler

1 Mickey Mouse PEZ holder

1 pink eraser

1 white eraser

1 fishing bobber

1 piece of a radio antenna

1 cracked candy cane

6 pen caps

1 film container with 43 blue beads

2 computer disks

3 mini–screwdrivers

1 mini–stapler

1 broken snail shell

1 plastic ring from a gum ball machine

3 red plastic pushpins

1 flashlight, doesn't work

4 short pencils, no erasers

1 roll of Scotch tape

3 butterscotch Life Savers

1 chain dog collar

3 rusty bolts

1 plastic bottle of white glue

1 Hacky Sack with a hole, blue beads leaking out

3 gray stones

2 pieces of green glass from the beach

1 pair of scissors with orange handles

1 mini Etch–A–Sketch on a key ring

1 eye off my old toy cat Fluffy

4 Star Wars action figures

1 broken camera

3 suction cups off of Garfield's paws

1 small, brown glass bottle

1 white shoelace

3 little seashells from Florida

1 round mirror from Mom's makeup

1 plastic bubble wand

2 root beer bottle caps

1 big nail

4 ribbons I won at YMCA camp

3 small nails, all rusty

1 old toothbrush

1 calculator

1 little roll of white string

1 plastic harmonica

1 short measuring tape

1 jingle bell off of my Christmas stocking

1 sand timer from a game

1 cork

1 wire key ring

1 pair of pliers

And then I stopped. There was still more stuff, but I was tired of writing. Plus I didn't want to use another piece of paper. Plus I felt like I was just wasting time.

I was almost ready to go and ask my dad for help. That would be dangerous, because of that K-I-A/D-I-A thing. That might be bad, but it would be better than never finding an idea at all.

But as I stared at all that stuff, I remembered something.

I remembered how I'd read in this kids' magazine about magnets. About how you can wrap wire around something made of iron. Then if you run electricity through the wire, it makes a magnet.

I pushed a bunch of things out of the way until I found the big nail. It was about four inches long. Then I found the roll of thin wire. Starting at the head of the nail, I began winding wire around and around, onto the nail. There wasn't that much wire. Still, I put about thirty turns on the nail before it ran out.

Then I grabbed the toenail clippers. I peeled some of the plastic cover off one end of the wire. Then I found the other end of the wire. I peeled some plastic off that end, too.

Now I needed power. I reached into the drawer and pulled out a big fat flashlight battery. I pressed one end of the wire on the top, and the other end on the bottom of the battery. Then I put the end of the nail near a small paper clip. And . . . nothing. Zero. Zilch.

I threw the nail and the wire and the battery into the drawer and started to shut it.

Then I thought, *Hey, you idiot! It's probably a dead battery—try again!*

I poked around in the drawer until I found one of those small boxy batteries, like the kind from a walkie-talkie. I hooked one end of the wire to each little button on the battery. I moved the nail next to a paper clip, and *zzip!* It jumped right onto the nail! And so did three other paper clips, and so did a bottle cap, and so did the fingernail file!

So then I looked at this wire and battery and nail. And I looked at the stuff dangling from the nail. And I said to myself, *Okay, but does this help with my science fair? This is just stupid stuff from my junk drawer.*

I looked at the science fair booklet again, at the question part, where it said:

What is the effect of_____**on**

_____**?**

So I asked. I asked myself,

"What is the effect of more batteries on the power of the magnet ?"

And then I asked myself,

"What is the effect of more wire on the power of the magnet ?"

And then I thought,

"What makes more difference, more wire or more batteries?"

And the great part was, I really wanted to know the answer!

You know how sometimes you can just see something in your head? Just see it like it was all right there? That's how it was.

I could see this big poster telling all about my idea. And another one telling how I tested my idea, and what results I got.

I could see these big supermagnets I made. They were all hooked up to batteries, humming like the lights at school. And my magnets were lifting up these heavy chunks of metal.

I could see myself at the science fair. I could see the judges listening to me explain everything. They were smiling.

I could see Kevin and Marsha. They were *not* smiling.

And I could see me sitting in my room. I was playing ZEE-SQUADRON STRIKE FORCE on my new Bluntium Twelve computer.

It was so simple.

All I had to do was make those things happen in real life. That's all.

CHAPTER SEVEN

Secrets and Spies

I learned a lot during that week before Christmas vacation.

I learned about the science fair and the grand prize. I learned that Mr. Lenny Cordo did not work for a circus. I learned that I wanted to win that Bluntium Twelve computer. I learned that sometimes my dad can be a K-I-A/D-I-A. I learned about the scientific method.

And I learned that just because you're in third grade, it doesn't mean you can't read some long words.

Like "electromagnets." That's the fancy name for the kind of magnets you make with wire and iron and electricity. That's something else I learned. Because the rest of that week before Christmas, I read all I could about magnets.

And another thing I learned is that a know-it-all can't really be a know-it-all. Nobody can know *everything*. There's too much. If you did know everything, your head would explode or something.

But I guess nobody ever told that to Kevin and Marsha. They really wanted to know everything, all the time.

But there was something they didn't know. And they knew they didn't know it.

They didn't know what my science fair project was.

At first, Kevin tried to pretend he didn't care. The day before vacation, we had to turn in our permission slips. Mrs. Snavin told us to bring them to her desk. I stood up, and Kevin got in line behind me. I could tell he did it on purpose.

Kevin tapped me on the shoulder. When I turned around, he gave me this fake smile and said,

"So, Jake, what are you doing your project on?"

I said, "I don't think I want to tell anybody."

He said, "Why not? It doesn't matter if people know. I'm doing mine on ants."

Kevin stared at me with his pale blue eyes. He didn't blink. He was waiting for me to tell. Especially since he had just told me what his project was.

But I just smiled and nodded. I said, "Ants. Yeah, ants are cool." And then I turned away because I had to hand my slip to Mrs. Snavin.

Kevin followed me back to my table. "So what's your project, Jake?"

I said, "I'm still kind of thinking about it."

Kevin said, "So what is it? What are you thinking about?"

I said, "I'll show you at the science fair."

Kevin pressed his lips together and made a mad face. Then he walked back to his own table.

You see, I'm a good secret keeper.

Two years ago, Abby broke a little china statue my mom had on a shelf. Mom loved it because she said it looked like Abby. That's why Abby loved it, too.

One day Abby pushed a chair over to the shelf and she took it down. When she started playing with it, the head broke off.

Abby brought it to me. She was crying. She was afraid she would get in big trouble. I used some white glue to put the head back on. I was very careful. You couldn't even tell it was broken. I put it back on the shelf. And I promised I would keep it a secret. And I did.

Of course, about a week later, Abby told Mom about the statue herself. And Mom wasn't even mad. Even so, I kept the secret.

And then there was the time a friend of mine was at the YMCA camp with me. In the middle of the night he woke me up. He whispered, "Jake . . . I . . . I wet my bed. What should I do?"

That's the kind of thing a kid can get a bad nickname for. So I helped him get the sheet off his bunk. It was a plastic mattress, so that was good. I got my extra sheet out of my trunk, and we put it on the mattress. Then we stuck the wet sheet under his bed and went back to sleep.

No one ever found out, and I never told.

And don't even try to guess which friend it

was, because I'm not telling. Ever. It's a secrct.

So I decided my science fair project was going to be a secret, too. Why tell anybody? Especially Kevin Young.

And Marsha? She never asked. She just snooped. And she was lousy at it. It was like I had radar. I could always tell when Marsha was trying to spy on me.

So I let her see me work, and I let Kevin see me, too. It was during our library period on the last day before vacation. I let Marsha see me check out a book on snakes.

Then I let Kevin see me looking at stuff about sharks in the encyclopedia.

Then I used *Encarta* to look up an article about weasels, and I left it on the computer screen a long time. I even took some notes. And Marsha saw me.

Then, ten minutes later, when Kevin was waiting at the printer, I printed out this article about rodents with a big picture of a rat. When I went to get it, Kevin handed it to me with a smile.

And I smiled back.

Near the end of the library time, I saw Kevin

and Marsha whispering together. They looked like they were arguing. Kevin probably thought my project was about rats and sharks, and Marsha probably thought I was studying snakes and weasels.

They didn't get my joke. What I did was study *them*. And I had discovered that Kevin reminded me of a cross between a shark and a rat, and Marsha was like a snake and a weasel.

What they didn't know was that in the bottom of my backpack, down in a safe dark place, I had three great books: *All About Magnets*; *Magnets You Can Make*; and *Winning Science Fair Projects*. And those three books were enough to help me win my new computer.

Because the best thing I learned that week before vacation was this: To be a good know-it-all, you don't have to know what anybody else is doing. And you don't need to know everything. You just have to know enough.

Plus it helps if you have a big drawer full of junk.

CHAPTER EIGHT

Dropouts

Then it was Christmas vacation. That's always been my favorite time of year. Where we live, there's almost always snow at Christmas. And there's nothing better than snow plus no school.

But this vacation was different.

On Christmas morning I was waiting at the top of the stairs with Abby. Was I thinking about all the presents under the tree in the living room? No. I was thinking about magnets.

And after the big Christmas dinner, and after Gram and Grampa went home, did I play with my new LEGO motor kit for the rest of the after-noon? No. I dug around in Dad's workshop. I was looking for wire and pieces of iron.

And it was like that all week. Every day I did some work on my project. I read my books. I made some drawings. I used the scientific method and I wrote things down.

One day I had Mom take me to the hardware store. We bought four big batteries. Each one was as heavy as a jar of peanut butter—a full one. We bought two of the biggest nails I had ever seen. They were about a foot long, and thicker than my pointer finger. And then we went to RadioShack and bought two big spools of thin wire.

That was what my vacation was like. When I wasn't working on my project, I was thinking about it.

I mean, I didn't work on it the whole week, not every second. One day I went sledding with Willie. We had a great time, and we didn't talk about our projects, not even once.

And I did build this amazing LEGO machine. Which Abby wrecked.

So even a big science fair project can't ruin Christmas. But it came pretty close.

The week after vacation, Kevin went from being a know-it-all to a show-it-all. You know how I worked to keep my project a secret? Kevin worked even harder to show and tell everyone about his. All the time.

If kids walked past Kevin's table, he would start telling all about his ants. And if they tried to walk away, he'd say, "And look what else I found out!"

Kevin worked on a big poster at the table by the windows. He just left it lying there for everyone to see. The poster was great, it really was—and it wasn't even half done.

In the gym on Tuesday, Kevin lay down on the floor by the wall. He started looking at some ants with a magnifying glass. They were in a long line, marching toward the door to the cafeteria. When kids came around, he told about how he had found out the way ants smell things. And how their eyes and jaws work.

And Kevin brought these amazing pictures. He took them with a digital camera. He printed them out on the color printer during library period. He showed them to everybody.

On Thursday I was waiting in line with Willie to buy ice-cream sandwiches. I said, "So did you start your project over vacation?"

He said, "Yeah, I got some done. But I'm not going to be in the science fair. And four other kids in my class, they're quitting, too."

I didn't understand. I said, "What do you mean?" Willie peeled back the paper and bit off a corner of his ice-cream sandwich. He said, "I quit the science fair. It's too much trouble. Besides, everybody knows Kevin's going to win."

I was still confused, and Willie could tell.

He said, "You've seen Kevin's stuff about ants, right? It's really good. And so is Karl Burton's stuff. In my class? His project is about simple machines. But I think Kevin's is better."

And then I got it. I got what Kevin had been doing all week.

I said, "Don't you see, Willie? Don't you see? That's what Kevin wants. He's been showing off his science project so kids like us will drop out. He set a trap, and you walked into it!"

Willie shrugged. "Yeah, I guess so. But what's the point? It wasn't any fun to work on."

Willie kept squeezing the ice cream out of the middle of his ice-cream sandwich so he could lick it off.

I said, "But what about the Bluntium Twelve? And a whole year of free Internet? Don't you want to win that?"

Willie shrugged again. "I mean, sure. That would be great. But I don't really *need* a new computer. And who wants to just try to beat Kevin all the time?"

That made me think. And I got madder and madder at Kevin. He didn't really break any rules, but what he was doing didn't seem fair.

And I got mad at Marsha because she was as bad as Kevin. All week long she had been telling everyone about her project, too. She was going to prove that she could fool grass seeds into growing upside down.

And then I got mad at Mr. Lenny Cordo. I thought it was all his fault that everyone was so upset about the science fair. Everyone was going nuts about his new computers.

And then I got mad at Mrs. Karp and Mrs.

Snavin and all the other grown-ups. They were the ones who let Wonky's Super Computer Store talk them into this whole idea.

And when I ran out of other people to get mad at, I got mad at myself.

I had turned myself into a know-it-all. I had gotten as mean as Kevin and as sneaky as Marsha. I had practically ruined Christmas so I could win the big prize.

But, worst of all, back when Willie wanted to be my partner, what did I do? I sent him off on his own. I threw him into the shark tank with Kevin and into the snake pit with Marsha. Willie and I could have had fun working on a project. Together.

All Thursday afternoon my thoughts went around and around. I got sick of the whole mess. And I decided there was only one thing to do.

I was going to forget about Kevin and Marsha.

I was going to forget about Mrs. Karp and Mrs. Snavin.

I was going to forget about Mr. Lenny Cordo. And his Bluntium Twelve computer.

I was going to quit the stupid science fair, too, just like my best friend, Willie.

CHAPTER NINE

Sticking Together

After I talked with Willie on Thursday afternoon, I felt like quitting the science fair. I really did.

I didn't talk to anyone on the bus after school. When I got home, I went right to my room.

Books and papers were spread all over the top of my desk. I had big batteries and spools of wire and giant nails spread around on the floor. I had markers and poster boards sticking out from under my bed.

The more I looked at all that stuff, and the more I thought about Willie, the madder I got.

And right then, I knew I couldn't quit. I just couldn't. I couldn't let Kevin and Marsha push everyone out of the way.

Then I got an idea. I looked around on my desk until I found the science fair booklet. Then I read the rules again. And for the first time in three or four hours, I smiled.

On Friday morning, I had my dad drive me to school. That way, I got there about ten minutes before the buses. I didn't talk much in the car.

When we were almost there, Dad said, "So, how's the science fair coming? It's next week, right?"

I shook my head. "Nope. It's the week after. And I guess it's okay."

"Anything I can help with? I've never made electromagnets, but I think I understand how they work."

I smiled and said, "Thanks, but I'm supposed to do the work myself. It says that in the rules."

We pulled up at the front door of the school. Dad said, "I'm sure you're doing a terrific job.

But maybe I could at least look things over."

I said, "Sure. That'd be good."

Dad leaned over and gave me a kiss on the cheek. "Have a great day, Jake."

I went into the office and asked Mrs. Drinkwater for permission to go to my room before the first bell. Mrs. Drinkwater is the school secretary. She's a good person to know. Even though Mrs. Karp is the principal, I think Mrs. Drinkwater runs my school most of the time. Because if you want to find out anything, you talk to Mrs. Drinkwater. Unless you're in trouble. Then you talk to Mrs. Karp.

When I got to my room, Mrs. Snavin was sitting at her desk using a calculator.

I guess my shoes were too quiet, because when I said, "Mrs. Snavin?" she jumped about a foot and let out this little squeal. "Oooh!—It's you, Jake. That gave me a fright."

I said, "Sorry, Mrs. Snavin. But I have to talk with you. You know Willie, my friend in Mrs. Frule's class? I want to be partners with him for the science fair."

Mrs. Snavin frowned. "The fair is the week

after next. I think it's a little late to be choosing up partners ."

I reached into my backpack and pulled out the science fair booklet. I said, "It doesn't say anywhere in here that you have to pick partners by a special time. It just says that you have to sign up on time, and it says you can work by yourself or with one partner. And Willie and I both signed up before Christmas."

Mrs. Snavin was still frowning. "Why has it taken this long to decide you want to work together?"

I said, "That's my fault. Willie wanted to be partners right at the start, but I said no. But now I want to. So will it be okay?"

Mrs. Snavin took a deep breath and let it out slowly. She was looking through my booklet. "Well . . . it doesn't seem to be against the rules. So, it'll be all right. I'll get the master list from the office and change it later today."

I said, "Thanks, Mrs. Snavin." Then I went back to the side doors to wait for the buses.

Willie was on bus four, but it was a while before he got off.

"Hey, Willie! Over here!"

He saw me and waved. He moved through the crowd of kids to where I was waiting. "Hi, Jake!"

We walked into the gym, and I said, "Guess what?"

"What?" he said.

"I've got a new partner for the science fair."

Willie looked at me and squinted. "What do you mean? Who?"

I grinned. "You! You're back in the science fair. You're my partner!"

Willie said, "No way!"

And I said, "Way! I talked with Mrs. Snavin already, and it's not against the rules or anything."

Willie smiled this smile that almost covered his whole face.

Then the smile stopped, and he squinted again. "But you said you wanted to work by yourself."

I said, "Yeah, but now I don't. I wasn't having much fun, either."

The first bell rang, and everyone began to move for the doors.

I said, "Tell you what. Get a pass to go to the library for lunch recess, and we can talk about it, okay?"

Willie said, "Yeah . . . okay. See you in the library." And then he smiled his big smile again. It's a great smile.

When you have a partner to work with, and it's a good partner, everything is more fun. It just is.

After Willie and I talked at the library we decided to work on the magnets. He had been making a project about how different balls bounce. It's because Willie loves basketball and almost every sport. He's not very good at sports, but he still loves them. So he wanted to observe Ping-Pong balls, golf balls, tennis balls, and basketballs bouncing. Then he wanted to guess why they bounced in different ways, and then try to prove it.

It was kind of an interesting idea, but Willie hadn't done much with it.

When I told him about the electromagnets, he got all excited. "You mean a regular nail turns into a magnet?"

I said, "Yeah, only I've got two giant nails this

long! And you know at a junkyard? They have electromagnets on the end of a crane that can pick up whole cars, and when they shut off the power, BAM, the whole car falls to the ground!"

Then I told him about everything we had to do. And Willie got more and more excited. He said he would ask his mom if he could come over on Saturday. Then we could work all day on it.

"That'll be great. And there's one more thing," I said. "I've been keeping the project a secret. Especially from Kevin and Marsha."

Willie nodded slowly and began to grin. "Yeah. I like it. That means we know something that they don't know, right?"

See what I mean? How Willie got the idea right away?

Me and Willie are like that. We're good partners. We laugh at the same kinds of stuff, and when he needs help or I need help, we stick together.

Like magnets.

CHAPTER TEN

Teamwork

You know how people say "two heads are better than one"? Well, it's true, especially if the other head is Willie's head.

When he came over to my house on Saturday morning, we got right to work. First, I showed Willie what I had written down. And I told him how it was my idea to see what made a magnet more powerful: more wire or more batteries. I had the idea, but I hadn't a guess about it yet. In the scientific method, that's called the hypothesis.

Willie looked at the stuff, and he looked at my notes. Then he said, "More electricity makes an electromagnet stronger than more wire."

I said, "How do you know that?"

Willie shook his head. "I don't. That's our hypothesis. 'More electricity makes an electromagnet stronger than more wire.' We have to prove whether that's true or false."

See what I mean about two heads? In a minute, Willie had a big part of the problem all worked out. I wrote the hypothesis in our notebook. Then came the fun part. I know that might sound weird, but making those electromagnets was really fun.

We talked and we argued about stuff, and we tried six different ways of winding wire on the nails. And Willie figured out a great way to keep track of how much wire we were using.

We decided to put 150 feet of red wire onto one of the nails. We would put 300 feet of blue wire onto the other nail. That was Willie's idea, too, to put twice as much wire onto the second nail. That way, if more wire makes a stronger magnet, maybe the blue magnet would be twice as strong.

We started winding wire onto one of the nails.

We kept the wire pulled really tight. It was harder than I thought it would be. And if I'd had to do it all by myself, it would have been really boring.

By lunchtime we had only finished the nail with the red wire, the short wire.

For lunch we had chicken noodle soup and grilled cheese sandwiches. Dad made lunch because Mom and Abby were at the mall taking some clothes back. Gram had given Abby a sweater that went all the way down to her knees. It made her look like a Munchkin.

Dad said, "It's been pretty quiet up there. How's it going?"

Willie said, "We've been winding wire around a nail."

Dad said, "If it's taking too long, you could bring your things down to the workshop. I bet I could figure out how to make the nail spin around. That way, you could just hold the spool of wire and it would almost wind itself. Sound good?"

Willie started to nod his head, but I said, "That sounds great, Dad, but we'd better do the second nail like we did the first one. They should look the same way."

I felt a little sorry for my dad. He really wanted to help. It was hard for him to keep out of the way.

Then I said, "But when we're done winding the second nail, would you look at them for us?"

Dad said, "You bet. Just give a holler when you need me."

And I could tell it made my dad feel good to be invited.

When Willie and I finished winding the wire, we looked in one of the books to see how to hook the batteries together. And that's when I called my dad. Because if you hook big batteries together wrong, it can start a fire. And it said in the rules that if anything might be dangerous, ". . . an adult should be present."

Dad was great. He didn't try to change anything we were doing. He didn't say we should wind the wire some other way. And instead of being a K-I-A/D-I-A and telling us how to hook up the batteries, he made us think about it. Then we had to tell him how we wanted to do it.

We told him, and Dad said, "That's exactly right. You guys have got it all figured out." And then he left. Mom would have been proud of him.

Willie and I decided our first trial should be with just one battery. So we hooked the wire from each end of the red magnet onto the battery—one wire to the positive terminal and the other to the negative terminal.

But we didn't have anything to lift with the magnet. So we unhooked the wires and went downstairs and into the kitchen.

I said, "We need something that's made of iron or steel."

And Willie said, "And we have to know how much it weighs. Because it said in the science fair booklet to measure everything. So we have to measure the weight of what we pick up."

I opened the door to the basement, but Willie said, "Wait a minute."

Willie's been to my house so many times, he knows where everything is. He opened the pantry, and right away I knew what he was doing. He was going to get some cookies. But instead he grabbed a can off a shelf and said, "Tuna!"

"Tuna?" I said.

"Yeah," said Willie. "Tuna. This can of tuna weighs one hundred and seventy grams. And this can of soup weighs three hundred and five grams. And the cans are made of steel! Here, take some."

So I grabbed eight cans of soup, and he grabbed four cans of tuna.

If I told you every step of our experiment, it would make you crazy. About how we tried two batteries on the red magnet. And then tried to see if we could pick up a can of soup with the flat end of the nail. And how we used duct tape to stack two cans on top of each other so we could try to pick up two cans. And how we hooked the two batteries up to the blue magnet and then tried to lift soup again. And how we wrote down everything we tried. And then how we hooked up all four batteries and . . . but like I said, if I just told it all, you'd go nuts. Because me telling it wouldn't be as fun as really doing all this stuff with Willie, and he was cracking jokes and making faces, and coming up with all these good ideas.

It was a great afternoon. And when Willie's

dad showed up to take him home, our science fair experiment was practically finished. I mean, we still had a ton of work to do. And posters to make. And conclusions to write.

But Willie and I knew what we knew, and we knew why we knew it.

And the best part? The best part was that all afternoon, I didn't think about Kevin or Marsha or Mr. Lenny Cordo or his Bluntium Twelve computer system. Not once. It had been an afternoon of pure fun.

Which is what science is supposed to be in the first place, right?

Right.

CHAPTER ELEVEN

Winners

Then came the weekend before the science fair. Willie and I spent all Saturday and Sunday finishing our posters. We planned what we would say to the judges. We planned how to explain our conclusion.

We also had to be ready to explain our method. That's the part where we tested our idea. Judges can ask any questions they want about any part of the project. So you know what you have to be? You have to be a know-it-all, at least about your own project. Unless you have a good partner like Willie. Then you can be a know-about-half.

Willie and I were ready. We even remembered to buy four new batteries so the magnets would work just right.

On the Tuesday of the science fair, we brought our project to the school gym at five o'clock in the afternoon. That was part of the rules. We had an hour and a half to get everything ready. Then the judging would start at six thirty.

The gym was like a pot of water on a stove. The whole place felt like it was humming and bubbling, getting ready to boil over.

Kids were everywhere. And so were parents. Both my dad and Willie's dad came along to help us hang up our posters. Willie's dad had gone to an office store for us. He got one of those tall cardboard fold-up things. It was just the right size to hold our three posters.

There were numbered tables in rows up and down the floor, and there was a list of names by the door. Next to every name there was a number, and ours was forty-five.

Table number forty-five was a good one, right along the back wall. Except that it was next to table number forty-six. And table number forty-six was Kevin Young's table.

It was hard not to look at Kevin's stuff. He had three posters, just like ours. Except his didn't look like ours.

We had used markers to write the biggest words on our posters. We had used colored pencils and crayons to make our drawings. We had written out our words by hand.

Not Kevin. All the writing on his posters had been printed out from a computer. And so had his pictures. All the papers and letters and pictures had been glued onto Kevin's posters.

We had glued some things onto our posters, too. We had some drawings, and a great picture of a junkyard electromagnet holding up a crushed car. It's hard to glue stuff right, so some of our pictures had some little bumps and ridges in them. And so did our writing papers.

Not Kevin's. I don't know how he did it, but every picture and all his writing was glued down perfectly flat.

My dad looked at Kevin's posters. He nodded at Kevin's dad and said, "Great posters."

Kevin's dad looked a lot like Kevin. He had the same red hair and blue eyes. He smiled at my dad and said, "Thanks. We worked pretty hard on them."

See that? How Kevin's dad said "we"? I looked around at the other projects near us. And most of them looked like grown-ups had helped, too. It didn't seem very fair. All of a sudden I wished that I had let my dad help us. Because deep down, I still thought it would be nice to win that Bluntium Twelve computer.

Kevin looked over at our stuff once or twice. And I thought I saw him smile a little, but it wasn't a nice smile. It was a put-down smile.

But we had too much to do to think about Kevin for very long. We got our magnets wired up. We got our cans of soup and tuna stacked up. We laid out our notebooks and our method records.

And when everything was set up, we had forty minutes left over, so our dads took us out for hamburgers and chocolate shakes. The food was good, but Willie and I were pretty nervous.

At six thirty, the judges started. There were six of them, science and math teachers from the junior high school. First, they all just walked together up and down the rows of tables. Then they started at table number seventy-two, the last table. And we had to wait. And wait. And wait.

It took a long time for the judges to get to our row. Then it was another ten minutes before they got to Kevin at table forty-six.

It was good to hear the judges ask questions before it was our turn. And Kevin was good at answering them. He really was. He had done this experiment making ants learn how to go through a maze. He wanted to show that if ants can't smell, they get lost.

Ants leave something like an odor where they walk. And if one ant goes through the maze, it leaves a trail so others can follow. So after one ant went through the maze, Kevin let another one go, and it followed the same path. Then he painted the maze with lemon juice, let it dry, and let another ant go. The second ant got lost, so Kevin proved his hypothesis was right.

It was a good project. Even if Kevin did get help from his dad.

Then it was our turn. This lady judge started. She asked Willie to explain what we wanted to prove. Willie pointed at our posters and told how electromagnets work, and how we wanted to see what made the bigger difference, more wire or more power. He was great. Willie smiled, and he sounded like he was having fun. Because he was. And I could tell the judges liked that.

Then it was my turn. I had to explain our method. I took it slow, step by step. And while I talked, Willie hooked up the red magnet to two batteries and lifted up two cans of tuna. Then he added two more batteries and picked up four cans.

Then Willie took over talking. I hooked up two batteries to the blue magnet, the one that had more wire on it. And with two batteries, the blue magnet would pick up four cans! And with four batteries, it picked up eight cans of tuna.

I could tell that the judges liked what we were doing. Our results were different from what we had thought they would be, but we explained it all in our conclusion just right. We used the scientific method. It was a good experiment.

Kevin was watching, too. But I couldn't tell what he was thinking. He didn't smile or frown. And he hardly even blinked.

Then it was over. And it felt great. I looked at Willie, and he had that smile on his face, the really big one. And right then, I knew I didn't care if we won anything or not.

The judges moved on. Then it was time for more waiting, a lot more waiting. So Willie and I went to look around.

There was a lot of neat stuff to see. There were projects about cameras, about fruit, earthworms, carbon dioxide from plants, fruit flies, fossils, hot air balloons, soap bubbles, different kinds of sand, and a really great one on electric guitar sounds. And tons more.

We found Marsha's table, but we didn't go over. That's because she looked sad, and kind of mad, too, like she might start crying or yelling or something. Her posters looked great. There was this upside-down cake pan inside a box with a window cut in one side. The pan was hanging above a little lightbulb. I could tell from the posters that the pan had some grass growing from it.

Willie said, "What's wrong with her?"

I shrugged and didn't say anything. But I thought I knew why. Maybe it was because if you always feel like you have to be the best, it's hard. Because a lot of the time, someone else does just as well or even better.

Anyway, we kept walking. We looked at all the third-grade projects. And after I saw them all, I knew which one was going to win. There wasn't any question about it.

About a half hour later, it was time for the announcements. Everyone went into the auditorium. Willie and I sat in the tenth row, and our dads sat behind us. Mr. Lenny Cordo was there, and all the computer boxes were stacked up on the stage. It was pretty exciting.

The judges announced the fifth-grade winners first. Ellen Stone won the grand prize. She'd done the project about the electric guitar sounds. And second place went to Mark Nixon for a project about temperature and soap bubbles.

The fourth-grade winner was Charles LeClerc.

He had studied the hardness of different kinds of rocks. And second place went to Amy Martin's project about veins in leaves.

Then it was time for the third grade. My dad put his hand on my shoulder and gave a little squeeze. And the winner was . . . Pete Morris. Just like I knew it would be.

Pete had done this project about insect eggs and how different daylight hours make the eggs hatch. IIe had found some praying mantis eggs. He'd put some lights on a timer and had made the eggs hatch two months early. It was like he'd tricked them with the light. And there was this big glass box with about twenty baby praying mantises walking around on their little green legs.

The great thing was that Pete had started his project back in October. That was almost three months before Mrs. Karp announced the science fair. He wasn't doing the project to try to be better or smarter than anyone else. And he didn't do it to try to win a new computer. He did it because he really wanted to figure something out. Like I said, Pete's a science kid.

Willie and I were standing up clapping for

Pete. Then the head judge said, "And second prize in third grade goes to Phil Willis and Jake Drake for their project on electromagnets."

Then they called all of us up onto the stage, and we had to shake hands with the judges, and then with Mrs. Karp and Mr. Lenny Cordo. And Willie and I each got a little silver trophy that said:

SECOND PLACE
FIRST ANNUAL
DESPRES ELEMENTARY SCHOOL
SCIENCE FAIR

It was the best thing I ever won. And it wouldn't have been half as fun without Willie there, smiling his biggest smile at me.

We went back to the gym to take our project apart. Kevin and his dad were there at table forty-six. His dad looked kind of mad.

But Kevin didn't. He said, "Nice trophy."

I said, "Thanks. I thought your project was really good."

Kevin said, "I guess. Too bad you didn't win first place."

I said, "Yeah."

But really, I didn't think it was too bad. I was happy with second place. And here's why.

You see, Pete's project was the best. He would have won no matter what. And second place? Maybe I could have won second place all by myself. But I don't think so. Willie did a lot to make the project better. Plus we had fun. Plus we did it all ourselves.

The best part about the science fair was that suddenly, it was all over. I didn't have to think about it anymore. I didn't have to keep track of all those papers and batteries and pieces of wire.

When we took everything apart, Willie kept the blue magnet, and I took the one with the red wire. Whenever I open my junk drawer now, there it is.

But the trophy is on my shelf. I keep it there to remind myself that there's one thing I never want to be again. Ever. And that's Jake Drake, Know-It-All.